Surfer the Seal

Library of Congress Cataloging-in-Publication Data

Burton, Jane.
    Surfer the seal / by Jane Burton. — North American ed.
      p.   cm. — (Baby animals growing up)
    Includes index.
    Summary: Depicts a seal in its early life as it grows, plays, and learns to feed itself.
    ISBN 0-8368-0210-1
    1. Seals (Animals)—Juvenile literature. 2. Seals (Animals)—Development—Juvenile literature. [1. Seals (Animals) 2. Animals—Infancy.] I. Title. II. Series: Burton, Jane. Baby animals growing up.
QL737.P6B9117 1989b
599.74'8—dc20
                                                        89-11368

This North American edition first published in 1989 by

Gareth Stevens Children's Books
7317 W. Green Tree Road
Milwaukee, Wisconsin 53223, USA

Format © 1989 by Gareth Stevens, Inc. Supplementary text © 1989 by Gareth Stevens, Inc. Original text and photographs © 1988 by Jane Burton. First published in Great Britain in 1988 by Macdonald & Co. Ltd.

Editors: Patricia Lantier and Rhoda Irene Sherwood
Cover design: Kate Kriege

Printed in the United States of America

1 2 3 4 5 6 7 8 9 95 94 93 92 91 90 89

**Baby
Animals
Growing
Up!**

Surfer the Seal

JANE BURTON

Gareth Stevens Children's Books
MILWAUKEE

Rona comes ashore on the nursery beach to give birth to her pup. As soon as Surfer is born, she nuzzles him, learning his smell.

Rona has to help Surfer to get his milk by pushing him toward the right place with her flipper. After a little while Surfer goes to sleep among the rocks. The wind dries his coat and makes it fluffy.

Two days old

Rona has gone into the sea for a rest. She likes to sleep in the water rather than on the rocky beach. But Surfer stays on the beach. He is skinny and has no fat, or "blubber," to keep him warm. But Rona is fat indeed.

The tide comes in, and Surfer crawls further up the beach. The waves wet him, but the water does not get through to his skin. His thick fur is waterproof and soon dries again.

Rona never swims far away but watches from the waves. Surfer will soon be hungry again. When he wakes up, he wipes the pebbles from his face with a flipper and calls to her.

Seven days old

Rona's milk glands are full again; it is time for another feeding. But Rona comes ashore too near Skerry and her pup. The cows squabble and lunge at each other. Rona might bite the pup if he goes near her.

Each cow can tell her pup by its smell, but sometimes pups go to the wrong cow and get a nasty shock. Instead of feeding it, the cow bites the pup and chases it away. By the time Rona and Skerry finish bickering, Surfer is very hungry. He wails at Rona to hurry up.

Ten days old

Rona rolls over so Surfer can feed. Her milk
is rich, and Surfer is getting fat. Already he
weighs twice as much as when he was born.
But while Surfer gets fat, Rona gets thin! She
has not eaten a thing since Surfer was born.

While Surfer feeds, Rona sleeps and never sees Skerry come ashore to feed Eddy.

Surfer is full and shuffles away up the beach. The scab on his head shows he has already had one painful lesson with Skerry. The wound is healing fast, but he takes no more chances.

Settling down among the rocks, Surfer gets ready for sleep. He licks the last milk from around his teeth. If Skerry comes near, Rona will wake up and chase her off. Surfer is safe.

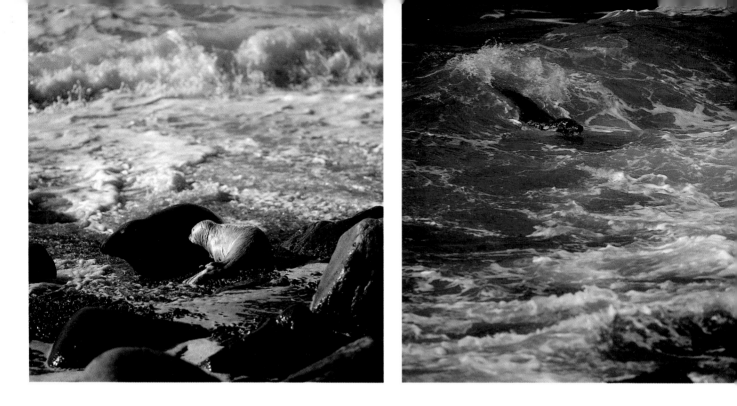

Twelve days old

The tide is coming in fast. Huge waves pound the nursery beach and crash on the rocks. Surfer, hungry as usual, rushes into the surf to meet Rona and nearly gets swept away.

Rona tries to protect Surfer, but the water pulls him past her and drags him out to sea. He can swim, but not very well, and he is not fat enough to live long in the cold water. Rona swims alongside, guiding him back to the shore but away from the dangerous rocks.

Mother and pup ride the crest of a big wave. It dumps them high up on the shingle. The foaming surf rushes back to join the next wave, nearly dragging Surfer with it. He clings to the shifting pebbles until the water drains away. Then following Rona, he hauls up the beach to safety. On the warm cobbles above the high-tide line, he rolls and squirms to dry his coat.

Fifteen days old

Orkney, Surfer's father, swims in the breakers with the two cows. He is uninterested in the pups and does not look after them. He is interested only in their mothers. Skerry keeps herself between him and Eddy, just in case.

Orkney follows Rona onto the rocks. At first she puts on a big show of not liking him. He wants to mate with her, so he is not put off by her display of bad temper. He looks pleased with himself. Surfer stays high up on the beach, out of harm's way.

Sixteen days old

Rona comes ashore five or six times a day to feed Surfer. All this time she eats nothing. She is getting thin, while her pup is a barrel of fat. Today she feeds Surfer for the last time and goes on a fishing trip to feed herself again.

Surfer feels deserted by Rona. He moans a bit, but he's so fat he can do without food for a while. He has put on so much blubber that he is three times as heavy as when he was born. He lolls around the beach and explores the rock pools when the tide is out.

Eighteen days old

It is nearly winter. Surfer's blubber keeps him warm in the coldest sea or the worst weather. But on the sheltered beach, it is warm in the sun, even in winter. Surfer gets too hot!

Surfer could stay cool in the sea, but he has started to molt and doesn't like to get wet just now. At the top of the beach is a cave where it is cool. Surfer goes into the cave to cool off.

Four weeks old

Surfer has shed most of his fluffy white baby fur and his next coat is mottled gray, like a grown-up seal's. Now he must find his way to the sea and learn to feed himself. He has nobody to show him what to eat. He tries eating seaweed and pebbles, but they are not good seal food!

In the rock pools Surfer finds crabs and prawns and shore fish that are easy to catch. These are good to eat.

All the time Surfer is out of water, his eyes cry salt tears. They stream down his face instead of down inside his nose. They wet his fur and make him look sad.

Six weeks old

Surfer goes out to sea to dive for food. His streamlined shape zips through the water like a torpedo. He swims like a fish but doesn't breathe like one. He often surfaces for air, then quickly dives again, especially when he nears a big seal that might bite him!

One year old

Now Surfer spends most of his time at sea, but sometimes he hauls out onto one of the secret beaches. Rona and Orkney and other big seals come there to bask at low tide. As the tide comes in, the seals haul further up the beach. At high tide, there is no beach left, so they all swim away.

23

Four years old

Surfer is big now but still not grown-up. He's not as
big as Orkney yet. He joins a gang of other young bulls.
 In one place below a cliff, pounding waves get sucked
down, then boil up in a seething whirlpool. The young
bulls play in the dangerous white water. Seals are
powerful swimmers, so the youngsters just have fun
in the torrent.

Sometimes Surfer and Eddy swim at each other
with snapping jaws — but only in play.   They
won't really fight until they are bossy grown-ups.
   When Surfer is tired of playing he wanders off to
calmer water to sleep. He hangs in the water like a
bottle, bobbing gently on the swell. His blubber
keeps him warm in the cold sea.

Six years old

Surfer has spent the years swimming from island to island, fishing a few days here, loafing a while there. Now he returns to the nursery beach to watch what's going on. Rona and Skerry are there, and so are several young cows, all with their new white-coated pups. A new boss bull is also there. Surfer had better keep out of the big bull's way for this year. Next year, or the year after that, it will be Surfer's turn to be the boss of one of the nursery beaches on an island in the North Sea.

Fun Facts About Seals

1. The largest seal is the Southern Elephant Seal, which lives in the sub-Antarctic waters off South America. The male may reach a length of 21 feet (6.4 m) long and may weigh up to 8,000 pounds (3,600 kg). This seal ranks second in size only to whales among all sea mammals.

2. Every spring, seals go to their breeding grounds, called rookeries, to find mates and to have young. Most rookeries are on islands.

3. Human beings are the seal's greatest enemy. They hunt the seal for fur or hides. The next greatest enemy of the seal is the Killer Whale. Killer Whales are medium-sized, sometimes reaching 30 feet (9 m) long.

4. Members of the seal order having flippers have existed for about 20,000 years.

5. Some seal species can descend to a depth of more than 1,000 feet (300 m) in the sea.

6. The Guadalupe Fur Seal, the Ribbon Seal, the Caribbean Monk Seal, and the Hawaiian Monk Seal are species of seals placed on the list of threatened mammals of the United States.

7. All seals have a layer of blubber 1 to 6 inches (2.5 to 15 cm) thick. It helps keep them warm and gives them energy when they can find no food.

8. Seals belong to the order of animals called *Pinnipedia*, as do sea lions and Walrus. *Pinnipedia* comes from two Latin words that mean, roughly, "feather-footed."

For More Information About Animal Life

Listed below are books, magazines, and a videocassette that will provide additional interesting information about seals and other sea life. Check your local library and bookstore to see if they have them or if someone there will order them for you.

Books
Elephant Seal Island. Shaw (Harper & Row Jr.)
Jack, the Seal, and the Sea. Aschenbrenner (Silver Burdett)
Sammy the Seal. Hoff (Harper & Row Jr.)
The Sea World Book of Seals and Sea Lions. Evans (Harcourt Brace Jovanovich)
Seal. Hoffman (Raintree)
Seals. Martin (Rourke)
The True Story of Corky the Blind Seal. Irving (Scholastic)
The White Seal. Kipling (Childrens Press)
The World of Seals. Saintsing and Allan (Gareth Stevens)

Magazines

Chickadee
Young Naturalist Foundation
P.O. Box 11314
Des Moines, IA 50340

Owl
Young Naturalist Foundation
P.O. Box 11314
Des Moines, IA 50340

National Geographic World
National Geographic Society
P.O. Box 2330
Washington, DC 20013-9865

Ranger Rick
National Wildlife Federation
8925 Leesburg Pike
Vienna, VA 22184-0001

Videocassette
Seals. Doubleday Multimedia.

Things to Do

1. Surfer learns a painful lesson after Skerry hits him on the head for getting too close to her and her pup. Think of a time when you learned a painful lesson and describe the experience in a short paragraph.

2. After Surfer comes in from the sea, he rolls on the beach and stays in the sun until his fur is dry. Make a list of other animals that bask in the sun to dry off after they have gotten wet.

3. Try to arrange a trip to the zoo to watch the seals move about and play. How do they act around each other? Do they seem to enjoy being with other seals? What kinds of noises do they make? Describe your observations in a short report.

4. Go to the library and check out one or two large picture books on seals. Try to determine the differences as well as the similarities in appearance. How many kinds or types of seals are there?

5. When Surfer gets too warm, he goes inside a nearby cave where it is cool. Would you know what to do if you were too hot? Name some ways you can think of to help keep cool.

6. Go to the library and find out the difference between a seal and a Walrus. Draw and color a picture of each that would show clearly the differences between them.

Things to Talk About

1. When Rona gives birth to Surfer, she immediately begins to nuzzle him and learn his smell. In what way is this process similar to what happens between human mothers and their babies?

2. Most of us never lose the need to cuddle and be cuddled. People without families often get animals so they have something to love. In fact, we now believe caring for animals and petting them improves people's physical and emotional health. How do you suppose this could be?

3. When Surfer is hungry, he calls out to his mother. Does she come right away? Does this pattern seem familiar to you? Why?

4. If Surfer would make a mistake and go near another pup's mother, she would probably bite or hit him. How do human beings normally behave when babies make mistakes or get lost? Explain.

5. Surfer's tremendous amount of blubber keeps him warm in winter. How do you keep warm in cold weather?

6. Surfer finally has to learn to feed and take care of himself. But he is still rather young and no one has really taught him what to do. Human children are reared differently. How are they taught to be independent? At what ages are they taught different skills?

7. Surfer's blubber keeps him warm in the cold sea water. What would it take to keep a human being warm in the freezing waters of the sea?

8. Surfer is an adult seal, or bull, at seven or eight years of age. How does this compare with humans at ages seven and eight?

Glossary of New Words

bask: to sunbathe; to warm up by staying out in the sun

bicker: to quarrel or disagree

blubber: the thick fat found in many sea mammals, which protects them against cold

bull: an adult male seal

cow: an adult female seal

crest: the highest point of a wave

flipper: a broad, flat limb adapted for swimming

haul: with relation to seals, to move by dragging and pulling the body with force

lunge: a sudden thrusting movement forward

mate: to join as a pair, male and female, in order to produce children

molt: to cast off or shed an outer layer of fur or skin, which will be replaced by a new growth of fur or skin

nuzzle: to push or rub with the nose; to lie close or snuggle

pebbles: small stones or rocks worn smooth and round by the action of water

pup: a young seal

seething: to surge, bubble, or foam as if boiling

shuffle: to move around by dragging or scraping the feet

squabble: a noisy quarrel about something that is usually not very important

surf: the waves of the sea which break on the beach

Index